21st Century Skills Library

ANIMAL INVADERS

WILD BOAR

Barbara A. Somervill

Cherry Lake Publishing
Ann Arbor, Michigan

CHERRY LAKE
Publishing

Published in the United States of America by Cherry Lake Publishing
Ann Arbor, Michigan
www.cherrylakepublishing.com

Content Adviser: Randy Westbrooks, U.S. Geological Survey

Photo Credits: Cover and page 1, ©Anita Huszti, used under license from Shutterstock, Inc.; page 4, ©imagebroker/Alamy; page 8, ©F1online digitale Bildagentur GmbH/Alamy; page 12, ©tbkmedia.de/Alamy; pag 13, ©North Wind Picture Archives/Alamy; page 17, ©Papilio/Alamy; page 20, ©Karin Lau, used under license from Shutterstock, Inc.; page 22, ©Adrian Sherratt/Alamy; page 25, ©blickwinkel/Alamy; page 26, ©AP Photo/Kathy Willens

Map by XNR Productions Inc.

Library of Congress Cataloging-in-Publication Data

Somervill, Barbara A.
 Wild boar / By Barbara A. Somervill.
    p. cm.—(Animal invaders)
 Includes index.
 ISBN-13: 978-1-60279-329-3
 ISBN-10: 1-60279-329-8
 1. Wild boar—Juvenile literature. I. Title.
 QL737.U58S66 2009
 599.63'32—dc22   2008035204

*Cherry Lake Publishing would like to acknowledge the work of
The Partnership for 21st Century Skills.
Please visit www.21stcenturyskills.org for more information.*

TABLE OF CONTENTS

CHAPTER ONE

WILD BOARS IN THE NEWS

A wild boar searches for food. Hungry boars have even been known to steal acorns from wood mice.

They are known by many names: wild pigs, wild boars, feral pigs, or feral hogs. They are also called razorbacks, Russian wild boars, European wild boars, and Old World swine. Whatever name is used, these creatures are real pests. They sometimes appear in the news. When they do, the news is not good.

In Texas, wild boars are causing major problems. The hogs are not just staying in forests or grasslands. The swine are invading Texas suburbs and cities. They eat anything they find, including crops. They have been known to raid chicken coops and feed on the chickens and eggs. They damage property when they tear up lawns. They even search through garbage. Just how many wild boars are there? Texas alone has approximately 1.5 million of the animals. Nearly half the states in the United States have feral pigs.

Feral pigs don't cause problems in just the United States. Many other countries around the world struggle with this invasive species, too. Wild boars are considered one of the most destructive animal invaders. They have certainly done their fair share of damage in Australia.

Australia's eastern forests have become a hog heaven. In the 18th century, European explorers brought hogs with them to feed their crews. Unfortunately, some pigs escaped into the wild. Australia had no natural **predators** to keep the pig population under control. Feral pigs multiplied in huge numbers. Today, Australia has a human population of slightly more than 20 million people—and an estimated feral pig population of 23 million. The feral pigs have spread to farms where they devour millions of dollars worth of crops every year.

In Europe, North Africa, and parts of Asia where wild boars or feral pigs are native, the pigs cause few problems. Those regions have natural predators, such as wolves and bears, to keep the population under control. Hunting by humans also helps keep feral pig numbers down. That isn't the case where hogs have been introduced. In the United States, Canada, Australia, New Zealand, and many other nations, wild boars cause problems. They invade farms, ranches, suburbs, and even parks. These animal invaders are making pigs of themselves. Humans, plants, and other wildlife are paying the price.

CHAPTER TWO

WILD BOAR OR FERAL PIG? SAME ANIMAL!

Wild boar piglets have striped fur that helps them blend in with their surroundings. This helps protect them from predators.

Wild boars look a bit like domestic farmyard pigs. They have pointed ears and flat snouts. They have large heads and broad shoulders. Their hair is coarse and the boars have ridges of long bristles going down their backs. The pigs vary in color. They may be brown, black, gray, blond, white, reddish, or any combination of colors. Black is the most common color.

As with domestic pigs, female wild boars are called sows. Male wild boars are simply called boars. Young boars are called piglets. The average adult wild sow weighs about 110 pounds (50 kilograms). Males are slightly larger. They weigh an average of 150 pounds (68 kg). Both males and females can vary greatly in weight and size.

One interesting feature of wild boars is their tusks. The upper tusks on males may grow to a length of 3 to 5 inches (7.6 to 12.7 centimeters). Tusks curl up and away from the mouth. They can produce a painful injury in human or animal flesh. Females have shorter tusks, but they are fiercely protective of their young. They are not afraid to chase off threats.

Feral pigs cannot sweat. To keep their bodies cool, they wallow in mud or take a swim. Mud also protects their skin from sunburn and insect bites. Because water and mud are important to wild pigs, the pigs usually

live by rivers, lakes, marshes, or other wetlands.

Wild boars are **omnivores**. This means they eat both plants and animals. The plants they eat change with the seasons. Springtime food may include sprouting grasses. Summer brings an increase in the amount of fruit eaten. Fall is the time for acorns and nuts. Pigs also feed on small mammals, lizards, insects, eggs, and **carrion**. Not being fussy eaters means that pigs can survive in any environment where they can find food.

Wild boars can breed throughout the year. Females can produce young

A group of female boars and their young drink at a pond.

when they are 6 months to 1 year old. Most sows, however, begin having babies when they are about 2 years old. Males mate when they are about 5 years old. They fight other males to win the right to mate with a sow.

Most births occur in the spring. The number of times a sow will give birth and how many piglets she will have can vary greatly. In general, a sow will have 2 litters per year. Each litter may have between 4 and 8 piglets. Boars have also been known to give birth more frequently in a year and to have larger litters. At birth, the piglets weigh between 1 and 2 pounds (0.45 and 0.90 kg). The piglets are born in a ground nest that the sow makes from twigs, grass, and leaves. They stay in the nest for about 1 week. After that, they follow their mother around. The babies drink milk from their mother until they are approximately 3 months old. Most piglets stay with their mother until they are 1 year old.

Females and their young travel around in a family group. Several family groups may gather together to form a sounder. A sounder may have as many as 50 animals. Adult males live alone. The average life span of a wild boar is about 8 to 10 years. But under the right conditions, wild pigs can live up to 27 years.

CHAPTER THREE

PIG INVADERS

Christopher Columbus first reached the Bahamas in 1492. Centuries ago, people didn't realize the risks of introducing animals into places where they didn't naturally live.

Sometime between 5,000 and 9,000 years ago, humans tamed wild pigs. The pigs became farm animals. Throughout Europe, Asia, and the Middle East, both wild and farm hogs provided meat and leather for human use.

In the 1490s, Christopher Columbus brought a small herd of farm pigs to the West Indies. Eventually, some pigs escaped into the wild. In the early 1500s, Spain's Hernán Cortés and Hernando de Soto brought more farm pigs with them as they explored southern North America. More pigs escaped into the wild. During the 1600s, the French explorer René-Robert Cavelier, Sieur de La Salle, also brought pigs to North America. As settlers arrived in the United States and Mexico, they also brought pigs for their farms. Over the years, many of those domesticated pigs escaped. The runaway pigs formed the base population for the millions of wild boars that now live in Canada, Mexico, and the United States.

More recently, European wild boars and Russian wild boars were brought to the United States to fill hunting preserves. In 1893, a New Hampshire preserve received 50 feral pigs from Germany. In the 1900s, Russian boars were introduced in North Carolina and California. The idea was to provide hunters with a population of boars to hunt within a controlled area. Unfortunately, the wild boars did not stay confined. Some escaped into the wild.

Today, wild boars are known to exist in 23 U.S. states. There may be populations of feral pigs in other states, but they have not been confirmed yet. In the United States, most wild boars live in southern states. They can be found from Florida to North Carolina, and westward as far as California and Oregon. Wild pigs also live in

21st Century Content

Wild boars were once native to Scotland. Their populations gradually shrank as people hunted the boars and cleared forestland. By the late 1500s or early 1600s, wild boars were extinct in Scotland.

Dealing with invasive species is a complicated global issue. Wild boars are pests in areas that they invade. But in regions where they naturally occur, the boars play a part in maintaining a healthy environment. Without any boars in Scotland, a specific type of fern plant grew out of control. The boars are one of the few animals that eat parts of this plant and control its spread.

In 2004, the Guisachan Wild Boar Project was launched. The project reintroduces wild boars into controlled areas in Scotland. Experts are studying the effect the boars have on the spread of the problematic plant. Do you think there are any risks to reintroducing wild boars in Scotland?

Wisconsin, New Hampshire, Vermont, and Pennsylvania. Hawaii also has its share of wild pigs. They were first brought there by sailors and left behind as a food source. They now cause a lot of damage in Hawaii's rain forests.

The spread of the wild boar has similar origins around the world. European explorers introduced pigs to South America, Australia, New Zealand, and many South Pacific islands. In each case, pigs were introduced as farm animals but eventually escaped from captivity to become wild boars. If only those explorers had known the trouble that wild boars would eventually cause!

PROBLEMS WITH WILD BOARS

In 2008, the whooping crane population was slightly more than 500. With numbers that low, the birds can't afford to compete with invaders such as wild boars.

A sounder of wild boars moves through Aransas National Wildlife Refuge on the coast of southeast Texas. The refuge is an important winter home for the endangered whooping crane. Along the shore, endangered sea turtles lay their eggs.

Hungry boars root through the wetlands looking for roots, nuts, and fruit. They rob the nests of ground birds, alligators, and sea turtles and eat their eggs. They compete with birds and mammals for food. They are upsetting the balance of nature in this important coastal stopping point for migratory birds.

In Australia, feral pigs eat their way through 22,046 U.S. tons (20,000 tonnes) of sugarcane a year. In areas where many sheep graze, the pigs kill and eat two out of every five newborn lambs.

In the Galápagos Islands, invasive pigs have run wild for more than 150 years. They eat endangered and rare plants. They feed on the eggs of endangered Galápagos tortoises, lava lizards, and green sea turtles. Wild pigs, along with other introduced wildlife, have played a major role in causing the extinction of several island species.

In Great Smoky Mountains National Park in eastern Tennessee, rangers have seen many changes caused by feral pig activity. Rooting for food has destroyed the **habitats** of three threatened animal species: the southern red-backed vole, the northern short-tailed shrew, and the red-cheeked salamander. The pigs have reduced plant cover in some areas by 80 percent. Forest litter from dead branches, leaves, and flowers is thinner. Changing the condition of the forest floor exposes more tree roots. This has led to the death of many trees. Because there is less ground cover, heavy rains cause soil **erosion** and a buildup of silt in streams.

21st Century Content

It is easy to list all the ways wild boars are inconvenient for people. But in some creative ways, boars may be helpful. Wild boars have an incredibly good sense of smell and sharp memory. Some people have put the pigs' natural abilities to good use. A European law enforcement officer has proved that a wild boar can be trained to search for buried explosives and drugs. Boars are able to smell objects several feet underground and can dig until they reach them.

Attacks involving explosives are a serious global issue in the 21st century. So is the illegal drug trade. Police and other law enforcement groups are always looking for new and better tools to help them prevent and solve crimes. Do you think boars will become a common police helper?

Contamination of crops, such as spinach, is a deadly reminder of how serious the wild boar problem is.

It is hard to put a dollar value on the loss of creatures such as Galápagos tortoises, green sea turtles, or red-cheeked salamanders. It is easier to measure the damage done by wild pigs to crops and livestock. The damages and losses to U.S. agriculture and property amount to more than $800 million per year. Much, but not all, of the damage involves pigs eating crops. But feral pigs don't have to eat crops in order to ruin them.

Experts believe a recent *E. coli* outbreak in California spinach was caused by feral pigs. The pigs may have passed feces containing *E. coli* bacteria in the spinach fields. As farmers watered the fields, the bacteria seeped into the soil and were taken up by the spinach plants. People who ate the spinach got sick, and a small number died. Farmers had to destroy their remaining crops.

Wild boars also carry diseases that affect other animal species. In all, feral pigs can carry more than 30 different diseases that harm cows, sheep, goats, and farm pigs. The pigs may carry pseudorabies, a disease that kills endangered Florida panthers. Feral pigs also carry the bacteria that cause Lyme disease in humans. The threat of disease from feral pigs is a real concern. In fact, feral pigs found on military bases are being vaccinated to prevent the spread of disease.

CHAPTER FIVE

SOLUTIONS IN THE WORKS

A farmer examines a field damaged by wild boars. The boars often disturb the ground and uproot plants when searching for food.

The first step in finding solutions to the problems caused by feral pigs is to figure out how large the problem is. But feral pigs are shy by nature and spend much of their time hidden from view. So the exact number of any feral population is not known. It is a bit easier to find wild boars and their nests on a small island in the Galápagos. It is very difficult to track down the pigs that roam freely in and out of the Florida Everglades, the swamps of Louisiana, or the heavily wooded regions of California. Land managers and scientists are struggling to get an accurate count of feral pigs in these areas.

In California and many other states, it is legal to hunt wild boars. In fact, hunting the pigs is encouraged. Hunting is one way to try to keep the population down. Game hunting alone, however, does not make much of an impact on the feral pig population. More than 85 percent of California's wild pig population roams on state

Tracking wild boars may be difficult, but experts are up for the challenge. Scientists in California use computer technology to help track wild pigs in the state. When someone hunts a pig, he or she must report where the pig was killed. Experts use this information and other sets of data to calculate how much territory the pigs have invaded in the past several years.

But just using high-tech tools isn't enough. Researchers must also be able to analyze this data in order to answer an important question: Where are the pigs headed next? By predicting where the pigs may spread in the future, researchers are trying to stay one step ahead of these animal invaders.

and federally protected land, as well as privately owned property. Hunting is not allowed in parks, preserves, and refuges. And few landowners encourage hunters on their property. So the pig population continues to increase, and efforts to control it have not been very successful.

One of the most successful efforts to get rid of wild boars took place on Santiago Island in the Galápagos Islands. The first attempts to control the pigs began in 1968. For more than 30 years, officials trapped, hunted, and poisoned wild boars that roamed the island. Their efforts finally paid off. After more than 150 years of living with invasive boars, Santiago Island is now free of the pigs. Officials are reintroducing some wildlife species that had become extinct on Santiago Island because of pig activities.

An effective program to bring wild boars under control takes money, planning, and effort. In Oregon, government officials have introduced a four-step plan that may cost more

It is not a smart idea to offer food to a boar or any other wild animal. You could get hurt or encourage the animal to seek food from humans.

than $1.3 million over 4 years and about $50,000 yearly once the program is established. First, laws have been established to control the release and tagging of farm pigs. Second, the public is being educated about the problem. Third, hunting and trapping of the wild pigs is being encouraged to help control the population. Finally, when pigs are removed from an area, the location will be monitored to make sure the pigs

A chef prepares a dish containing wild boar meat. Do you think wild boar will become more popular as a food?

don't return. This may seem like a lot of work and money for a bunch of pigs. But Oregon's agriculture and livestock industry is worth more than $3.6 billion per year. Compared to that, $1.3 million is cheap.

Feral pigs are also being trapped in the southwestern United States. In that region, some trappers have even gone into the wild boar meat business. They catch the pigs and have them slaughtered. They sell the meat in Europe and to a small but growing number of consumers in the United States. In a few years, wild boar might be available in the supermarket meat case.

What makes the wild boar such an amazing—and invasive—creature is its ability to adapt to different environments. Boars can survive in mountainous zones, forested regions, and other areas around the world. Humans have their work cut out for them if they hope to control the spread of these animal invaders.

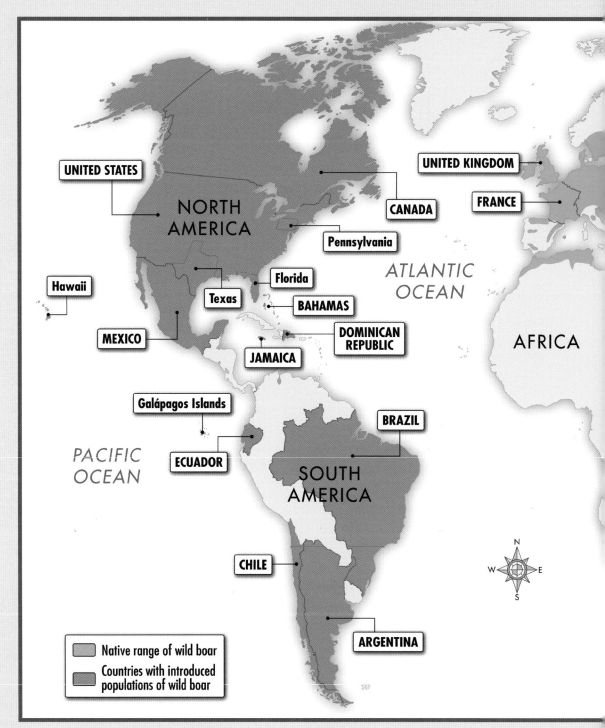

UNITED STATES

NORTH
AMERICA

UNITED KINGDOM

CANADA

FRANCE

Pennsylvania

ATLANTIC
OCEAN

Hawaii

Florida

Texas

BAHAMAS

AFRICA

MEXICO

DOMINICAN
REPUBLIC

JAMAICA

Galápagos Islands

BRAZIL

PACIFIC
OCEAN

ECUADOR

SOUTH
AMERICA

CHILE

N

W   E

S

Native range of wild boar

Countries with introduced
populations of wild boar

ARGENTINA

This map shows where in the world the wild boar

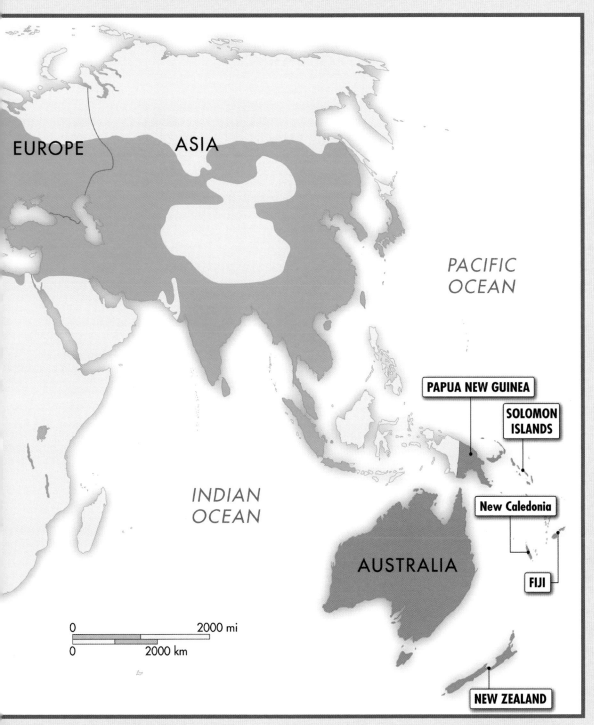

EUROPE

ASIA

PACIFIC
OCEAN

PAPUA NEW GUINEA

**SOLOMON
ISLANDS**

INDIAN
OCEAN

New Caledonia

AUSTRALIA

FIJI

0   2000 mi
0   2000 km

NEW ZEALAND

lives naturally and where it has invaded.

Glossary

carrion (CAIR-ee-on) rotting flesh of a dead animal

conservationists (kon-sur-VAY-shuhn-ists) people who work to preserve, manage, and care for the environment

endangered (en-DAYN-jurd) at risk of dying out completely

erosion (i-ROH-zhuhn) the wearing away of rock or soil by wind or water

extinction (ek-STINGT-shun) the condition of no longer existing; extinction occurs when all the members of a species have died out

feces (FEE-sees) the solid waste of an animal

feral (FIR-uhl) relating to a wild animal or describing a domestic animal that has returned to the wild

habitats (HAB-uh-tats) the places where an animal or plant naturally lives and grows

invasive species (in-VAY-siv SPEE-sheez) any plant or animal that is not native to an area but has moved into the region

omnivores (OM-nuh-vorz) animals that eat both meat and plants

predators (PRED-uh-turz) animals that hunt and kill other animals for food

swine (SWINE) pigs or hogs

vaccinated (VAK-suh-nay-tid) given an injection or dose of a special substance in order to make a human or animal immune to a disease

FOR MORE INFORMATION

Books

Banting, Erinn. *Galapagos Islands.* New York: Weigl Publishers, 2007.
May, Suellen. *Invasive Terrestrial Animals.* New York: Chelsea House Publications, 2006.

Web Sites

Feral Pigs
www.dnr.state.wi.us/org/land/wildlife/publ/wlnotebook/pig.htm
Visit this site from the Wisconsin Department of Natural
Resources to find out more about feral pigs

Wild Boar
www.invasivespeciesinfo.gov/animals/wildboar.shtml
Learn about the habits of wild boars and why they have become a nuisance

INDEX

ABOUT THE AUTHOR

Barbara A. Somervill writes children's nonfiction books on a variety of topics. As a writer, she has had many different cool careers—teacher, news reporter, author, scriptwriter, and restaurant critic. She believes that researching new and different topics makes writing every book an adventure. When she is not writing, Ms. Somervill plays duplicate bridge, reads avidly, and travels.